Scottish Shortbread

Scottish Shortbread

Mary Macdonald

illustrated by

Christopher Corr

HAMLYN

ACKNOWLEDGEMENTS

Art Director Jacqui Small

Designer Louise Leffler

Executive Editor Susan Haynes

Editor Elsa Petersen-Schepelern

Production Controller Melanie Frantz

Illustrator Christopher Corr

First published in 1995 by Hamlyn
an imprint of Reed Consumer Books Limited
Michelin House, 81 Fulham Road, London SW3 6RB
and Auckland, Melbourne, Singapore and Toronto.
Text copyright © 1995 Reed International Books Limited
Illustrations and design copyright © 1995 Reed International Books Limited
ISBN 0 600 58479 8
A CIP catalogue record for this book is available at the British Library.
Printed in Hong Kong

NOTES

Both metric and imperial measurements have been given in all recipes.
Use one set of measurements only and not a mixture of both.
Standard level spoon measurements are used in all recipes.
1 tablespoon = one 15 ml spoon   1 teaspoon = one 5 ml spoon
Eggs should be size 3 and milk full fat unless otherwise stated.
Ovens should be preheated to the specified temperature – if using a fan
assisted oven, follow the manufacturer's instructions for adjusting
the time and the temperature.

Contents

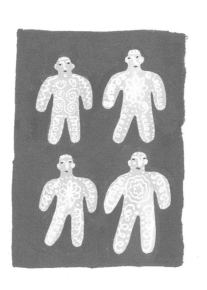

Introduction

Scotland is the source of some of the finest of British produce – berries and beef, salmon and game – and of course that nectar of the gods, so closely linked with the country that the very word 'Scotch' has come to mean whisky.

But Scottish cooks, wonderful though they are at making the most of that splendid produce, have reached their pinnacle in baking. And of all the cakes and breads, biscuits and scones which issue in fragrant procession from Scottish ovens, it is Shortbread which has achieved worldwide fame. Boxes and tins of this delicious, rich, biscuity pastry are sent around the world at Christmas and New Year as an integral part of the traditional festive season.

This book includes the two basic recipes '2-4-6' and '2-4-8' (2 oz sugar to 4 oz butter to either 6 or 8 oz flour). The jury is still out on which is the better of the two. Also included are many traditional or unusual variations on that original: Pitcaithly Bannocks, Petticoat Tails and delicious Shortcakes of all kinds. Cook, taste, enjoy – and judge for yourself.

Scottish Shortbread

This is a delicious, traditional shortbread.
It is perfect for the first-time shortbread maker – it is
very simple, and requires no kneading.

125 G /4 OZ BUTTER
50 G /2 OZ CASTER SUGAR
250 G /8 OZ PLAIN FLOUR
SALT
CASTER SUGAR, FOR DUSTING

1 Cream the butter and sugar together until very soft.

2 Beat in the flour and salt.

3 Roll out to 2.5 cm/1 inch thickness and put in a greased
18 cm/7 inch round flan tin. If it will not roll well,
it can be pressed into the tin by hand.

4 Prick well with a fork and lightly mark into sections
with the back of a knife.

5 Bake for 45-60 minutes in a preheated oven at
120°C (250°F) Gas Mark ½
until golden brown.

6 If liked, dust with caster sugar before serving.

Makes 8 slices

Butter Shortbread

This shortbread is richer than most, because there is less flour and more butter than in traditional recipes. It should be handled very carefully when hot, because all that butter means the shortbread is inclined to be brittle.

125 G/4 OZ PLAIN FLOUR
50 G/2 OZ CORNFLOUR
50 G/2 OZ CASTER SUGAR
125 G/4 OZ BUTTER

1 Sieve the flour and cornflour together. Add the sugar and rub in the butter. The mixture will become crumbly at first, but continue rubbing in with your fingers until it clings together in heavy lumps.
2 Turn on to a board or working surface, lightly dusted with flour or cornflour, and knead lightly.
3 Roll out to a 20 cm/8 inch circle and place on a greased baking sheet. Prick all over the top with a fork, mark into 8-10 portions and flute the edges with your fingers.
4 Bake in a very moderate oven at 170°C (325°F) Gas Mark 3 for 30-35 minutes until the shortbread is cooked but not browned.
5 Leave the shortbread on the baking tray for about 10 minutes, then lift off with a fish slice and place carefully on a wire rack to cool.
Makes 8-10

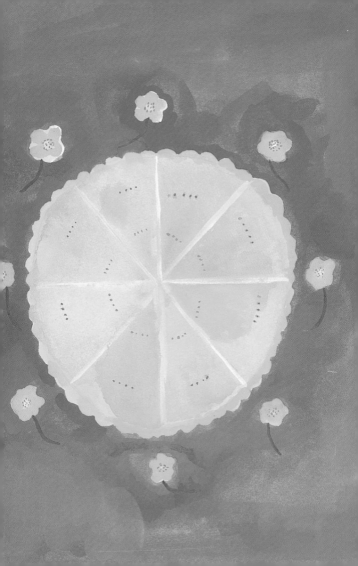

Traditional Scottish Shortbread

*The addition of semolina gives extra crispness and a
melt-in-the-mouth texture. For added crunch and flavour,
sprinkle chopped hazelnuts over the shortbread before baking.*

50 G/2 OZ CASTER SUGAR

125 G/4 OZ UNSALTED BUTTER, SOFTENED

150 G/5 OZ PLAIN FLOUR

25 G/1 OZ FINE SEMOLINA

1 TABLESPOON CHOPPED HAZELNUTS (OPTIONAL)

CASTER SUGAR, FOR DREDGING

1 Cream together the sugar and butter until pale, light and fluffy.
Stir in the flour and semolina, using a fork. Press the mixture into an
18 cm/7 inch round sandwich tin. Smooth the surface using a palette
knife and decorate the edges using a fork. Prick all over with a fork
and sprinkle with caster sugar. Sprinkle with chopped hazelnuts
(if wished) and press lightly into the surface.

Bake in a preheated moderate oven at 160°C (325°F) Gas Mark 3 for
about 1 hour. the shortbread should be pale but just beginning to
colour. Cool in the tin for 15 minutes, then mark into 8 wedges.

3 Carefully ease out of the tin and cool on a wire rack.

Store in an airtight container.

Makes 8 wedges

Rich Scottish Shortbread

*Carved wooden shortbread moulds are becoming rare
and expensive, but you can use a fluted flan ring instead – whic
will stop it spreading during baking. Decorated with a sprig of
heather tied up with tartan ribbon, shortbread makes
an attractive Christmas gift.*

250 G /8 OZ PLAIN FLOUR
125 G /4 OZ RICE FLOUR OR GROUND RICE
125 G /4 OZ CASTER SUGAR
A PINCH OF SALT
250 G /8 OZ UNSALTED BUTTER, SLIGHTLY SOFTENED

1 Sift the two flours (or flour and rice), sugar and salt into a mixing
bowl. Cut up the butter and rub it into the dry ingredients. When it
starts to bind, gather it into a ball with one hand. Knead it on a lightly
floured board until it is a soft, smooth and pliable dough.

2 Place a 20 cm/8 inch flan ring on a greased baking tray and put in
the dough, pressing it out evenly with your knuckles. With the back o
a knife, mark it into 6 or 8 triangles. Prick all over with a fork in a nea
pattern. Chill for 1 hour to firm it up before baking.

3 Bake in the centre of a preheated oven at 150°C (300°F)
Gas Mark 2 for 45-60 minutes or until the shortbread
is a pale biscuit colour but still soft.

4 Remove from the oven and leave to cool and shrink before
removing the ring, then dust lightly with caster sugar.

Makes 6-8 pieces

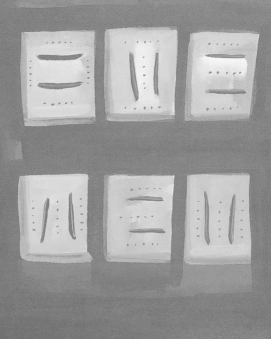

Mrs Beeton's Scotch Shortbread

No – Mrs Beeton's shortbread does not contain Scotch.
A common mistake, and one which the Scots would be
happy to correct!

1 KG/2 LB FLOUR
500 G/1 LB BUTTER
125 G/4 OZ POUNDED LOAF SUGAR (USE CASTER SUGAR)
15 G/½ OZ CARAWAY SEEDS
25 G/1 OZ SWEET ALMONDS, BLANCHED AND CUT INTO SMALL PIECES.
A FEW STRIPS OF CANDIED ORANGE PEEL

Beat the butter to a cream, gradually dredge in the flour and add the
sugar, caraway seeds and sweet almonds. Work the paste until quite
smooth, and divide it into 6 pieces. Put each cake on a
separate piece of paper, roll the paste out square to the thickness of
about 2.5 cm/1 inch, and pinch it upon all sides. Prick it well and
ornament with one or two strips of candied orange peel.
2 Put the cakes into a preheated and bake at 180°C (350°F)
Gas Mark 4) for 25-30 minutes.
Makes 6 cakes

Wholemeal Shortbread

*Wholemeal shortbread has a delicious, nutty, 'brown' taste –
and it's just an extra bonus that the wholemeal flour makes this
shortbread good for you as well!*

90 G/3½ OZ PLAIN WHOLEMEAL FLOUR
15 G/½ OZ RICE FLOUR
75 G/3 OZ UNSALTED BUTTER
2 TEASPOONS MUSCOVADO SUGAR

1 Sift the flours into a bowl and the bran remaining in the sieve.
Stir well. Rub in the butter until the mixture resembles fine
breadcrumbs, and stir in the sugar.

2 Using your hands, bring the mixture together to form a smooth
dough and then knead lightly.

3 Pat the dough out to fit a lightly greased, shallow, 18 cm/7 inch
square tin and smooth the top. Prick with a fork and cut
into 12 fingers.

4 Bake in the centre of a preheated oven at 180°C (350°F)
Gas Mark 4 for 20-25 minutes. Retrace the markings and leave
to cool in the tin. Remove and store in an airtight tin.
It will keep fresh for up to 10 days.

Makes 12 pieces

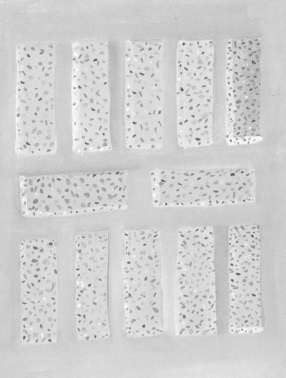

Pitcaithly Bannocks

In Scotland, bannocks were broken above the bride's head as she stepped over the threshold of her new home, to bring good luck and good health to her household.

150 G/5 OZ PLAIN FLOUR

25 G/1 OZ GROUND RICE

125 G/4 OZ BUTTER, CUT INTO PIECES

75 G/3 OZ CASTER SUGAR

25 G/1 OZ CHOPPED MIXED PEEL

25 G/1 OZ UNBLANCHED ALMONDS, FINELY CHOPPED

1 TABLESPOON MILK

CASTER SUGAR, TO SPRINKLE

1 Put the flour and ground rice in a bowl. Add the butter and rub in with the fingertips until the mixture resembles fine breadcrumbs. Stir in the sugar, peel and almonds. Add the milk and work with the hands until the mixture clings together. Divide the mixture in half.

2 Knead one piece of dough lightly until smooth. Place inside an 18 cm/7 inch fluted flan ring on a baking tray and press out evenly. Remove the ring carefully and repeat with the remaining dough. Prick both rounds all over with a fork.

3 Bake in a preheated oven at 180°C, 350°F Gas Mark 4 for 35 minutes, or until lightly coloured. Leave for 5 minutes, sprinkle with caster sugar and cut each round into 8. Cool on a wire rack.

Makes 2 bannocks

Tropical Pitcaithly Bannocks

A recipe from tropical Australia, where shortbread makers are advised to make shortbread in the early morning or late evening. One Scots-born cook bakes hers at midnight! Salted butter is usually used in the tropics because it preserves the butter longer.

175 G/6 OZ FLOUR

50 G/2 OZ RICE FLOUR

50 G/2 OZ CASTER SUGAR

1 TABLESPOON CARAWAY SEEDS

125 G/4 OZ SALTED BUTTER

TO DECORATE:

2 TABLESPOONS CANDIED PEEL OR

ORANGE GLACÉ ICING AND

2 TABLESPOONS HUNDREDS AND THOUSANDS

1 Mix the flour, rice flour, caster sugar and caraway seeds together, then add the butter and knead until the dough forms a ball. Press out carefully into a 23 cm/9 inch round.

2 Crimp the edges and prick the top all over with a fork. Sprinkle with the candied peel, if using.

3 Cook in a preheated oven at 180°C (350°F) Gas Mark 4 for about 30 minutes until golden.

4 When cool, ice with orange glacé icing and sprinkle with hundreds and thousands, if liked.

Makes 1 x 23 cm/9 inch round

Petticoat Tails

A favourite of Mary Queen of Scots. Some people say that its charming name is a corruption of the French 'petites gatelles' (little cakes). But you will see that the dough, before baking, looks frilled and pleated like a petticoat.

375 G/12 OZ PLAIN FLOUR

A PINCH OF SALT

2 TEASPOONS CARAWAY SEEDS

125 G/4 OZ CASTER SUGAR

175 G/6 OZ BUTTER

4 TABLESPOONS MILK

Sift the flour with the salt into a bowl. Mix in the caraway seeds and the sugar. Melt the butter in the milk, but do not overheat. Mix it into the flour and knead lightly. Roll out on a floured board into a round just over ½ cm/¼ inch thick.

2 Invert a dinner plate on top and cut around with a sharp knife. Using the forefinger of one hand and the forefinger and thumb of the other hand, pinch a fluted edge all round. Cut out a round in the centre of the cake with a tumbler and cut the surrounding circle into 8 wedges to make the 'petticoat tails'.

3 Line a baking sheet with parchment or greaseproof paper and place the biscuits on top. Bake in a preheated oven at 180°C (350°F) Gas Mark 4 for about 20 minutes or until crisp and golden.

Makes 9 pieces

Apricot-topped Almond Shortbread

A sumptuous concoction! Start with the recipe for Rich Scots Shortbread. Cut and cook as in the recipe for Shortbread Fingers then pile on the juicy apricots, top with clotted cream, and sprinkle with flaked almonds. Heavenly!

6 SHORTBREAD FINGERS (SEE PAGE 28),
MADE WITH THE RECIPE FROM
RICH SCOTS SHORTBREAD (SEE PAGE 12)
2 DROPS ALMOND ESSENCE OR ALMOND LIQUEUR
1 x 425 G/15 OZ CAN APRICOT HALVES
150 ML/¼ PINT CLOTTED OR EXTRA THICK CREAM
1 TABLESPOON FLAKED ALMONDS

1 Place the shortbread biscuits on 6 individual plates. Mix the almond essence or liqueur with about 2 tablespoons of the apricot juice and pour 1 teaspoon over each piece of shortbread to moisten slightly.

2 Spread the shortbread biscuits thickly with cream.

3 Cut the apricot halves into thin slices and arrange decoratively on top of the cream.

4 Arrange or sprinkle with flaked almonds and serve immediately with afternoon tea.

Makes 6

Festive Shortbread Biscuits

*This recipe was handed down to a Scotswoman in
East Africa by her Highland grandmother, but the decorations
are her own idea. She also suggests adding currants and
grated nutmeg to the mixture before baking.*

250 G/8 OZ FLOUR

75 G/3 OZ CASTER SUGAR

125 G/4 OZ BUTTER

1 EGG YOLK, BEATEN

1 TABLESPOON CREAM OR MILK

A PINCH OF SALT

Sift the flour and salt into a bowl, add the caster sugar and rub in the
butter. Add the egg yolk and cream and mix thoroughly. Place the
mixture on a board and knead until smooth. Roll out the
dough to 5 mm/¼ inch thick and cut into festive shapes
with biscuit cutters.

Put the biscuits on to a greased baking sheet and bake in a moderate
oven at 180°C (350°F) Gas Mark 4 for 15-20 minutes.

3 For birthdays or tea parties, these biscuits may be decorated with
almonds, pistachios, glacé cherries or crystallized violets,
before baking or, when cool, spread with glacé icing
and sprinkled with hundreds and thousands.

Makes 6-10

Shortbread Fingers

Shortbread traditionally comes in round cakes with fluted edges cut into triangles. But Shortbread Fingers – delicious rectangles shortbread – are just as popular, especially with children.

ONE QUANTITY OF MIXTURE FOR
RICH SCOTS SHORTBREAD
(SEE PAGE 12)

1 Press the mixture into a greased 20 cm/8 inch square tin.

2 With a sharp knife, cut it across right down to the base, into strips 2.5 cm/1 inch wide and then across into fingers of equal length. Prick through neatly to the base with a fork.

3 Chill for at least 1 hour to firm it up before baking.

4 Bake in the centre of a preheated oven at 150°C (300°F) Gas Mark 2 for 45-60 minutes or until it is a pale biscuit colour but still soft.

5 Remove from the oven, cut through again in the same slits, but leave to cool before loosening the edge and turning out upside down on a sugared, greaseproof paper.

6 Separate the fingers, turn right side up, leave to cool on the sugared paper, and store when cold.

Makes 16 fingers

Ginger Shortbread

*Ground ginger gives this shortbread an unusual
Christmassy taste.*

250 G/8 OZ BUTTER, SOFTENED
125 G/ 4 OZ CASTER SUGAR
250 G/8 OZ PLAIN FLOUR
2 TEASPOONS GROUND GINGER
CASTER SUGAR, FOR SPRINKLING

1 Mix the butter and sugar together on a clean surface. Gradually
work in the sifted flour and ginger to form a dough.
Knead until smooth.
Roll the dough out to 5 mm/¼ inch thick and cut into rounds with
medium scone cutter, or any shaped cutter. Place on a baking sheet.
3 Bake in a preheated oven at 160°C (325°F) Gas Mark 3
for 15-20 minutes until golden brown and sprinkle with caster sugar
while still warm.
4 Cool on a wire rack before serving, or store in an airtight tin.
Makes about 36

Hazelnut Shortbread

*Rich, buttery, shortbread fingers flavoured with
roasted hazelnuts*

230 G/8 OZ BUTTER, SOFTENED
60 G/2 OZ SOFT LIGHT BROWN SUGAR
170 G/6 OZ PLAIN FLOUR
30 G/1 OZ RICE FLOUR OR GROUND RICE
110 G/4 OZ HAZELNUTS, ROASTED AND CHOPPED IN A
LIQUIDIZER OR PROCESSOR

1 Grease and line a 30.5 x 20.5 cm/12 x 8 inch shallow cake tin.
2 Cream the butter and sugar together. Fold in the flour, rice flour or
ground rice and nuts. Knead the mixture to form a firm shortbread
dough, and press evenly into the tin with a palette knife.
3 Bake at 170°C (325°F) Gas Mark 3 for 35-45 minutes or until
golden and firm to the touch. Mark into 24 fingers.
4 Leave to cool in the tin for 15 minutes, then transfer to a wire rack
to finish cooling. Store in an airtight container for up to 4 days.
Makes 24

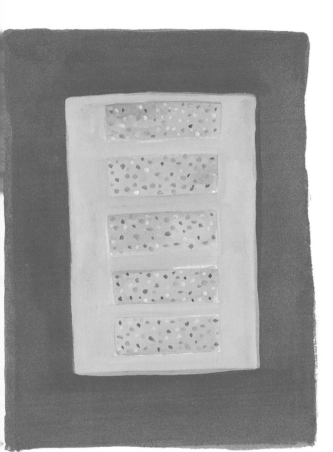

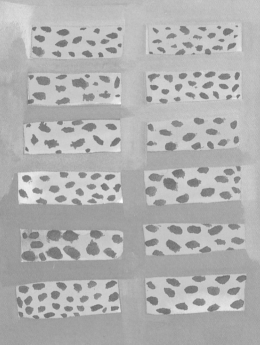

Cherry Shortbread

*Shortbread Fingers bursting with juicy glacé cherries
and dusted with icing sugar.*

250 G/8 OZ PLAIN FLOUR
125 G/4 OZ ICING SUGAR
PLUS EXTRA FOR DUSTING
125 G/4 OZ CORNFLOUR
250 G/8 OZ BUTTER AT ROOM TEMPERATURE
175 G/6 OZ GLACÉ CHERRIES,
RINSED, DRAINED AND CHOPPED

1 Sift together the flour, the icing sugar and the cornflour.
Beat the butter until it is soft, then gradually beat in the flour
mixture. Stir in the chopped cherries and mix to a firm dough.
Knead the dough in the bowl until it is smooth.
2 Press the dough into a greased and floured 28 x 18 cm/11 x 7 inch
baking tin and smooth the top. Prick the shortbread all over
with a fork.
3 Bake in a preheated oven at 160°C (325°F) Gas Mark 3
for about 40-50 minutes.
4 Cut the shortbread into fingers and dredge with icing sugar.
Leave in the tin to cool.
Makes about 20

Lemon Spice Shortbread

*Grated clementine, satsuma or orange rind makes a
good alternative to lemon rind.*

175 G/6 OZ PLAIN FLOUR
½ TEASPOON GROUND CINNAMON
A PINCH OF SALT
1 TEASPOON FINELY GRATED LEMON RIND
50 G/2 OZ CASTER SUGAR
125 G/4 OZ BUTTER

1 Sift together the flour, cinnamon and salt. Stir in the lemon
rind and sugar. Rub in the butter until the mixture clings together.
2 Roll out the dough to 5 mm/¼ inch thickness and cut into
fingers 2.5 x 7.5 cm/1 x 3 inches. Transfer to a greased baking tray.
3 Prick neatly with a fork and bake in a preheated oven at
160°C (325°F) Gas Mark 3 for 15-20 minutes.
4 Cool on a wire rack and dredge with caster sugar.
5 Serve immediately, or store in an airtight container.
Makes about 22 biscuits

Shortbread Date Slices

*You will find that this home-made version is much
better than the shop-bought variety.*

FOR THE FILLING:

250 G/8 OZ STONED DATES

1 TABLESPOON HONEY

1 TEASPOON GROUND CINNAMON

150 ML/¼ PINT COLD WATER

2-3 TEASPOONS LEMON JUICE

FOR THE SHORTBREAD:

175 G/6 OZ BUTTER

75 G/3 OZ CASTER SUGAR

175 G/6 OZ SELF-RAISING FLOUR

175 G/6 OZ SEMOLINA

1 Put all the filling ingredients into a pan and simmer until soft.

2 Melt the fat and sugar for the shortbread in another pan.
Add flour and semolina and mix well. Put rather less than half the
shortbread mix into a Swiss roll tin and spread with a palette knife.

3 Put all the date mixture over this and spread the rest of the
shortbread on top. Cook in a preheated oven at 190°C (375°F)
Gas Mark 5 for about 25 minutes.

4 Cut into slices or squares and serve as a hot pudding with
custard or cold at teatime.

Makes 8

Chocolate Shorties

Shortbread for the chocoholic!

125 G/4 OZ BUTTER
50 G/2 OZ SOFT BROWN SUGAR
125 G/4 OZ SELF-RAISING FLOUR
2 TABLESPOONS COCOA POWDER
15 G/½ OZ HAZELNUTS, CHOPPED

1 Beat the butter and sugar together until light and fluffy.
Sift in the flour and cocoa and mix well.

2 Using dampened hands, form into balls the size of a walnut
and place on baking sheets lined with non-stick paper.

3 Bake in a preheated oven at 180°C (350°F) Gas Mark 4
for 15–20 minutes, until lightly browned; the mixture
will crisp as it cools.

4 Carefully remove the shortbread from the paper
with a palette knife when cool.

Makes 12

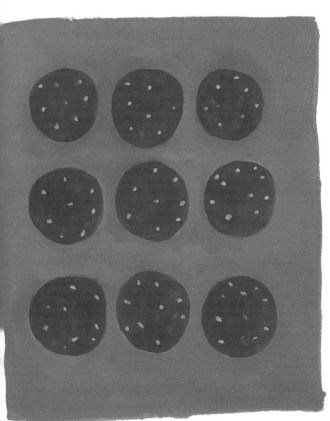

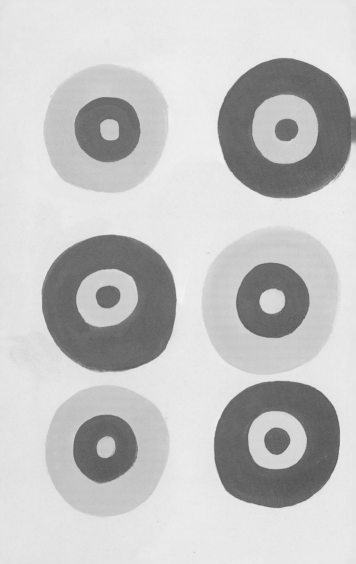

Shortbread Wheels

Party-time shortbread!

150 G/5 OZ PLAIN FLOUR
50 G/2 OZ CASTER SUGAR
125 G/4 OZ BUTTER
1 TABLESPOON COCOA POWDER
1 TABLESPOON DRINKING CHOCOLATE POWDER

1 Sieve 140 g/4 ½ oz of the flour into a bowl. Add the sugar. Rub in the butter until it is crumbly, and divide the mixture in half. Add the remaining flour to one half and the cocoa and drinking chocolate to the other half. Knead each portion well with your fingers to form a smooth dough. Turn on to a working surface lightly dusted with flour. Roll out each portion to 6 mm/¼ inch thick and from each cut out 6 cm/2 ½ inch circles. Out of these circles, cut two more circles, one 4 cm/1 ½ inch and one 2 cm/¾ inch, making three in all.

2 Separate these circles and place on greased baking sheets, alternating the colours so that in half the biscuits you have two plain and one chocolate circle and in the others you have two chocolate and one plain circle. Bake in a preheated oven at 180°C (350°F) Gas Mark 4 for 12 minutes. Leave on the sheets for 2 minutes, then remove with a palette knife and cool on a wire rack.

3 Variation: roll out the dough into 2 rectangles and place one on top of the other. Roll up like a Swiss roll, cut into thin slices and place on greased baking trays.

Makes 14

Lemon Shortbread Men

*Use a cutter for Gingerbread Men to stamp out these shapes,
and make their eyes and buttons with dried or crystallized fruit
chocolate drops, liquorice or candied peel.*

175 G/6 OZ UNSALTED BUTTER

75 G/3 OZ CASTER SUGAR

250 G/8 OZ FLOUR

25 G/1 OZ RICE FLOUR OR GROUND RICE

GRATED RIND OF 1 LEMON

A LITTLE CASTER SUGAR FOR SPRINKLING

CANDIED PEEL, DRIED FRUIT, LIQUORICE OR CHOCOLATE DROPS

A GINGERBREAD MAN CUTTER

1 Cream the butter until soft. Add the sugar and beat until pale and
fluffy. Add the grated lemon rind, mix in the flour and rice
flour or ground rice until the mixture binds together.
Knead lightly to form a smooth dough.

2 Roll out 6 mm (¼ inch) thick on a lightly floured surface.
Cut out gingerbread-man-shaped biscuits, re-rolling the trimmings
as necessary. Place the Shortbread Men on baking trays and
chill for 15 minutes.

3 Set the oven at 180°C (350°F) Gas Mark 4. Bake the biscuits for
15 to 20 minutes until pale golden and just firm to the touch.
Add the eyes and buttons, and cool on a wire rack.

Makes 5

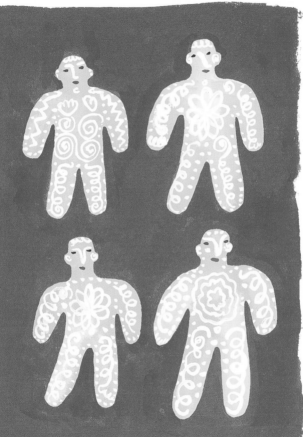

Fruit Shortcake with Fresh Nectarines

350 G/12 OZ PLAIN FLOUR, SIFTED

225 G/8 OZ SOFT BUTTER

100 G/4 OZ SOFT BROWN SUGAR

½ TEASPOON VANILLA ESSENCE

175 G/6 OZ CURD CHEESE

1 TABLESPOON HONEY

2 NECTARINES (OR OTHER FRUITS, SUCH AS APRICOTS OR PEACHES)

1 Place the flour in a large mixing bowl and rub in the butter. Stir in the sugar and the vanilla essence. Bring the mixture together and knead lightly. Divide in half. Roll out each half to form a 20 cm/8 inch round. Flute the edges with a fork.

2 Place on lightly-greased baking sheets and mark one round into 8 sections. Bake in a preheated oven at 160°C (325°F) Gas Mark 3 for 50-60 minutes until lightly browned. Remove from the oven. Cut through the sections on the marked round. Cool slightly, transfer to a wire tray and leave to cool completely before filling.

3 Cream the curd cheese and honey together. Peel, stone and chop one nectarine and add it to the curd cheese. Spread this mixture carefully on to the uncut round of shortbread.

4 Place the remaining shortbread wedges on the cheese mixture at an angle, overlapping slightly.

5 Thinly slice the remaining nectarine, without peeling it, and use to decorate the top of the shortcake.

Serves 8

Date and Apple Shortcake

FOR THE NUT PASTRY:

75 G/3 OZ BUTTER

40 G/1 ½ OZ DARK SOFT BROWN SUGAR

125 G/4 OZ WHOLEMEAL FLOUR

75 G/3 OZ BRAZIL NUTS, GROUND, AND 1 TABLESPOON CHOPPED NUTS

EGG WHITE

FOR THE FILLING:

3 TABLESPOONS APPLE JUICE

500 G/1 LB DESSERT APPLES, PEELED AND SLICED

125 G/4 OZ DATES, CHOPPED

1 TEASPOON GROUND CINNAMON

150 ML/¼ PINT DOUBLE CREAM, WHIPPED

1 Beat the butter and sugar together until softened. Stir in the flour and ground Brazil nuts and mix to a firm dough. Turn onto a floured surface; knead lightly until smooth.

2 Divide in half and roll each piece into a 20 cm/8 inch round. Brush one with egg white and sprinkle with the chopped nuts.

3 Bake on a baking sheet in a preheated oven at 190°C (375°F) Gas Mark 5 for 10-15 minutes until golden. Cut the nut-covered round into 8 sections while warm. Cool both rounds on a wire rack.

4 Place the apple juice and slices in a pan. Cover and cook gently for 10 minutes until just soft. Add the dates and cinnamon. Cool.

5 Spread the apple filling over the whole shortcake round, cover with the cream and the cut top.

Serves 8

Chocolate Cherry Shortcake

*This is a 'Grand Occasion' shortbread, suitable
for a special dinner party.*

125 G/4 OZ BUTTER

50 G/2 OZ CASTER SUGAR

150 G/5 OZ PLAIN FLOUR, SIFTED

25 G/1 OZ COCOA, SIFTED

300 ML/½ PINT DOUBLE CREAM, WHIPPED

350 G/12 OZ FRESH OR CANNED
BLACK CHERRIES, STONED

SIFTED ICING SUGAR FOR SPRINKLING

1 Cream the butter and sugar together until soft and creamy, then stir
in the flour and cocoa. Mix to a firm dough, turn on to a floured
surface and knead lightly.

2 Divide the mixture in half and roll each piece into a 20 cm/8 inch
round on a baking sheet.

3 Bake the shortbread in a preheated moderate oven,
180°C (350°F) Gas Mark 4 for 20 minutes.

4 Leave for 2 minutes, then cut one round into 8 sections.
Carefully slide both rounds on to a wire rack to cool.

5 Reserve 2 tablespoons of the cream. Mix the rest with the
cherries and spread over the chocolate round.

6 Arrange the cut sections on top and sprinkle with icing sugar.
Decorate with the reserved cream, and serve immediately.

Serves 8

American Strawberry Shortcake

The classic shortcake recipe – no doubt created by American descendents of Scottish frontierswomen.

250 G/8 OZ PLAIN FLOUR

1 TABLESPOON BAKING POWDER

½ TEASPOON SALT

50 G/2 OZ CASTER SUGAR

50 G/2 OZ BUTTER

ABOUT 150 ML/¼ PINT MILK

350 G/12 OZ RIPE STRAWBERRIES OR 300 G/10 OZ FROZEN BERRIES

150 ML/¼ PINT DOUBLE CREAM, WHIPPED WITH 1 TEASPOON CASTER SUGAR (OPTIONAL)

1 Sift the flour, baking powder and salt together and stir in the sugar. Cut in the butter with a pastry scraper or round-bladed knife.

2 Stir in just enough milk to make a soft dough. On a lightly floured board, pat – do not roll – the dough into a 30 cm/12 inch wide oblong. Cut out two 15 cm/6 inch rounds.

3 Lay the pastry rounds on a lightly greased baking sheet and bake in a preheated oven at 220°C (425°F) Gas Mark 7 for about 10 minutes, until risen and brown.

4 Reserve 10-12 of the best berries. Lightly crush or halve the remainder and spread on one shortcake layer. Spread on some of the cream. Add the second layer and 'frost' with the remaining cream. Decorate with the reserved berries, and serve.

Serves 4–6

Pineapple Meringue Shortcake

FOR THE SHORTCAKE:
300 G/10 OZ PLAIN FLOUR
¼ TEASPOON SALT
150 G/5 OZ BUTTER
200 G/7 OZ CASTER SUGAR

FOR THE MERINGUE:
2 EGGS, WITH THE YOLKS WHISKED SEPARATELY
AND THE WHITES WHISKED TO SOFT PEAKS
1 TABLESPOON FLAKED ALMONDS

FOR THE FILLING:
425 G/14 OZ CAN PINEAPPLE PIECES, DRAINED
150 ML/¼ PINT DOUBLE CREAM, LIGHTLY WHIPPED
A FEW GLACÉ CHERRIES

Follow Steps 1 and 2 of the recipe on page 51 for Chocolate Cherry
Shortcake, omitting the cocoa. Remove and place on a wire rack to
cool. Reduce the oven to 140°C (275°F) Gas Mark 1.

2 Whisk the egg whites, and whisk in the remaining sugar a
teaspoon at a time. Pipe or spoon rosettes of the meringue around the
edge of the shortcake. Sprinkle with almonds. Return to the cool oven
for 30 minutes, until the meringue is crisp. Rest 10 minutes on the
baking tray, then remove and cool on a wire rack.

Fold most of the pineapple into the cream and spread over the centre
of the cake. Decorate with the remaining pineapple pieces
and the cherries.

Serves 6-8

Index

Weights and Measures

In this book, both metric and Imperial measures are used.
When working from the recipes, follow one set of measures only,
and not a mixture of both, as they are not interchangeable.

Notes for American and Australian Users
In America, the 8 fl oz measuring cup is used. In Australia, metric
measures are used in conjunction with the standard 250 ml measuring
cup. The Imperial pint, used in Britain and Australia, is 20 fl oz,
while the American pint is 16 fl oz.

The British standard tablespoon, which has been used throughout this
book, holds 17.7 ml, the American 14.2 ml, and the Australian 20 ml.
A teaspoon holds approximately 5 ml in all three countries.

British	American	Australian
1 teaspoon	1 teaspoon	1 teaspoon
1 tablespoons	1 tablespoon	1 tablespoon
2 tablespoons	3 tablespoons	2 tablespoons
3½ tablespoons	4 tablespoons	3 tablespoons
4 tablespoons	5 tablespoons	3½ tablespoons

An Imperial/American Guide to Solid and Liquid Measures

Imperial	American	Imperial	American
Solid Measures		Liquid Measures	
1 lb butter	2 cups	¼ pint	⅔ cup
1 lb flour	4 cups	½ pint	1¼ cups
1 lb granulated		¾ pint	2 cups
sugar or caster		1 pint	2½ cups
sugar	2 cups	1½ pints	3¾ cups
1 lb icing sugar	3 cups	2 pints	5 cups
8 oz rice	1 cup		(2½ pints)

From mom & dad love
July 1995